Forge into new entrepreneurial territory.

Free Zone Frontier is a way of approaching your entrepreneurial career to bypass all competition and continually collaborate with other 10x achievers to build brand new areas of value creation.

Creating Great Free Zones

Free Zone Creativity

Competition-Free Frontiers

Instantly Invisible Advantages

Friction-Free Collaboration

Escaping Crowded Conformity

Everything's Collaborative

Extending The Frontier

Six Ways To Enjoy This Strategic Coach Book

Text **60 Minutes**	The length of our small books is based on the time in the air of a flight between Toronto and Chicago. Start reading as you take off and finish the book by the time you land. Just the right length for the 21st-century reader.
Cartoons **30 Minutes**	You can also gain a complete overview of the ideas in this book by looking at the cartoons and reading the captions. We find the cartoons have made our Strategic Coach concepts accessible to readers as young as eight years old.
Audio **120 Minutes**	The audio recording that accompanies this book is not just a recitation of the printed words but an in-depth commentary that expands each chapter's mindset into new dimensions. Download the audio at **strategiccoach.com/go/FZF**
Video **30 Minutes**	Our video interviews about the concepts in the book deepen your understanding of the mindsets. If you combine text, cartoons, audio, and video, your understanding of the ideas will be 10x greater than you would gain from reading only. Watch the videos at **strategiccoach.com/go/FZF**
Scorecard **10 Minutes**	Go to the Mindset Scorecard at the end of this book to score your Free Zone Frontier mindset. First, score yourself on where you are now, and then fill in where you want to be a year from now. Download additional copies at **strategiccoach.com/go/FZF**
ebook **1 Minute**	After absorbing the fundamental ideas of the Free Zone Frontier concept, you can quickly and easily share them by sending the ebook version to as many other individuals as you desire. Direct them to **strategiccoach.com/go/FZF**

Thanks to the Creative Team:

Adam Morrison

Kerri Morrison

Hamish MacDonald

Shannon Waller

Jennifer Bhatthal

Victor Lam

Margaux Yiu

Christine Nishino

Willard Bond

Peggy Lam

Free Zone Frontier

The most successful entrepreneurs are never satisfied with the status quo. They're always looking for opportunities to push beyond the boundaries of their industry and marketplace, into new territories where they can use their unique skills to create increasing value for their desired audience.

Break free from competition and, instead, collaborate with other 10x achievers to create totally "free zones" where no one else has yet ventured and growth is unlimited. This is the essence of entrepreneurism.

Cartoons by Hamish MacDonald.

Printed in Toronto, Canada. The Strategic Coach Inc., 33 Fraser Avenue, Suite 201, Toronto, Ontario, M6K 3J9.

This publication is meant to strengthen your common sense, not to substitute for it. It is also not a substitute for the advice of your doctor, lawyer, accountant, or any of your advisors, personal or professional.

If you would like further information about The Strategic Coach® Program or other Strategic Coach® services and products, please telephone 416.531.7399 or 1.800.387.3206.

Library of Congress Control Number: 2019912333
Author Academy Elite, Powell, OH 43065

Available via Audiobook and:
Print: 978-1-64085-832-9
Ebook: 978-1-64085-833-6

Contents

Introduction
Collaboration Bypasses Competition

You collaboratively combine your best capabilities and resources with others' to create entirely new entrepreneurial possibilities and payoffs that grow extraordinarily quickly in ways amazingly free of competition.

A newly discovered, uncontested area—a "Free Zone"— only stays new for so long before it becomes the new normal and fills up with numerous people in addition to whoever got there first.

So what does the discoverer of a Free Zone do once it becomes a known quantity that anyone can travel to?

Well, one option is to push past the frontier and continue further into uncharted territory to find another Free Zone.

What entrepreneurism means.

There can be all sorts of frontiers—including emotional frontiers, psychological frontiers, and intellectual frontiers—and new frontiers are constantly being created by people who feel limited by the established order under which they live.

Their capabilities can't come out, and who they are can't grow. So they say, "We're going to push out."

And this is essentially what entrepreneurism means.

The fundamental definition of entrepreneurism is taking any kind of resource from a lower level of usefulness and value to a higher level, both for yourself and others.

French economist Jean-Baptiste Say came up with this definition in the early 1800s. Entrepreneurs take something that isn't demonstrating value and raise its power so that it becomes valuable. And all of a sudden, they start attracting new consumers.

Seeing what others can't.

Anytime you entrepreneurially transform an existing situation by combining underproductive resources, you suddenly acquire capabilities for rapid and profitable growth that no one else can see or understand.

Entrepreneurism is seeing value in a possibility no one saw before and being willing to focus your capabilities on making that possibility into a reality—forging into a new Free Zone where there's no competition.

But this has an expiry date on it because the moment that a Free Zone becomes popular, the freeness of the zone decreases. Rules get established, and the exciting, abundant part of it disappears. And you have to do it all again.

There's always a tension between those who dwell in established areas and those who push the boundaries, but once entrepreneurs understand that their entire lives have to involve always pushing into new frontiers, they avoid becoming part of the establishment.

Indeed, entrepreneurs stop being entrepreneurs when they want to become the establishment of the new zone and live there permanently. The secret to being a constantly growing entrepreneur lies in always moving on to a new Free Zone that others can't yet see.

Competition depletes existing value.

Most stories of entrepreneurial success—mostly told by non-entrepreneurial outside observers—focus almost entirely on the isolation and negativity of cutthroat competition over opportunities, resources, and rewards that have already been created because of collaboration.

Collaboration creates entirely new kinds of value. Competition, on the other hand, always depletes existing value of its creativity, usefulness, productivity, profitability, and meaning.

Once collaboration has created a brand new industry, that industry fills up with competitors. This will soon take the value creation in the zone down to nothing because, for the competitors who have moved in, everything will be all about the price of what's being offered rather than about creativity and innovation.

So the individuals who created the great value in their collaboration have to move out of the Free Zone they created and think of what their next collaboration and Free Zone creation will be.

Creating new Free Zones.

For all of your entrepreneurial life that lies ahead, you can choose to use only new forms of collaboration to create bigger and better Free Zone Frontiers that are increasingly free of any kind of competition.

You can avoid all of the isolated competition you previously thought was the only way to be an entrepreneur, and focus your energies on expanding your limits and collaborating with other like-minded individuals to create brand new value far greater than what anyone involved would be able to create on their own.

The vast majority of entrepreneurs won't be up to this because they feel too locked into the fierce competition that defines their entrepreneurial lives.

But those entrepreneurs who are drawn to this idea immediately know that it's right for them and that they're going to start leaving energy-depleting competition behind and devoting their entrepreneurial lives to energizing, value-creating collaboration projects.

If this resonates with you and you're motivated, you'll learn to recognize rewarding opportunities all around you and that there's an abundance of rewards available when you're creating brand new value.

Entirely new territory.

You can always be extending the frontier of your capabilities outward into new zones of entrepreneurial achievement where you're free to grow beyond the control of existing conditions.

This is the very essence of what entrepreneurism is—the creation of a Free Zone Frontier. And it's available to any person on the planet who has the desire, imagination, and willingness to venture into new territory.

Chapter 1
Creating Great Free Zones

You're always mastering the process of combining existing unique capabilities into a new venture that is automatically competition-free.

Many entrepreneurs don't believe that being free of competition is a possibility so they don't bother having it as a goal. For them, the center of the universe is increasingly intense competition.

They don't see how being competition-free could be a skill. To them, that would be called "not making any money."

But the truth is that creating new Free Zones is possible and it's a skill, which means you'll get better and better at it the more you do it.

Already uniquely 10x.

If you're a successful entrepreneur, you've already created a uniquely successful business that, in a crucial aspect, is 10x better than most of your marketplace competitors.

What you're uniquely good at is working with people who have resonant mindsets, and you build capabilities and skills around that.

Your customers and clients aren't with you because of your product or service. It's because being with you is a transformative experience for them.

In order to move forward, you have to recognize that as a competitive entrepreneur, you're 10x better in some key competitive area. This is the unique value that you have to offer the marketplace.

You have to take ownership of your uniqueness to be part of this game.

Now you want to grow 100x.

Based on what you've already achieved, you can feel confident that you can multiply the value of your unique 10x capability to reach 100x if you link up with another, completely different 10x capability that needs your approach to create 100x superior value.

To create a new Free Zone, it takes two people who have already gone 10x, who are thinking 100x, and neither can go 100x by sticking with what they've already achieved.

You need to link up, and the linking up needs to be with someone whose capability is very different from yours. Combining similar capabilities won't do it. Similar is the territory of mergers and acquisitions, and in that, you might be able to go 2x or 3x, but not 100x.

To go 100x, you and your collaborator need to agree up front about who it is you want to be heroes to, who you want to create unique value for. You have to know who your target audience is and always have that on your minds.

You also both need to have a passion for creating a much greater value creation model than exists already.

Next step, competition-free.

No entrepreneur starts off in a Free Zone because you have to have a full dose of competition to understand what being competition-free is.

You've already learned how to grow your capabilities, teamwork, and results while facing competition, commoditization, and regulation on all sides. And now, you want to create an entirely new value creation breakthrough that's completely free of competition.

And through your superior competitive abilities, you've earned the right to now be competition-free.

You multiply them, they multiply you.

As you continually link up with different 10x capabilities, each new combination will multiply the opportunities and results of everyone involved.

The goal of going 100x triggers your recognition of what's needed to achieve it. You need to have that 100x frame of mind in order to figure out what collaboration has to happen.

Thinking 100x, you immediately know that the way you've done things so far just isn't going to cut it. You can't get there through competition, and that's a major purpose of the 100x mindset: you free yourself from competition in your mind because if you don't, reaching your goal will be impossible.

And once you free yourself from competition in your mind, you have a way of freeing yourself from competition in reality.

Thinking of going 100x can be compared to my plan for living to age 156: Having the goal in mind for the future changes how you think and operate *today*.

If you keep building capabilities, you'll eventually reach that 100x goal, but it will seem like a minor detail when it happens. The thrill comes from the fact that you're doing this totally new form of value creation without any competition. The real reward is the activity itself.

Expanding creativity and credibility.

Everything about your new collaborative activities will be easier and more enjoyable than the competitive pressures you used to face, and each new achievement is going to expand your confidence, creativity, and credibility.

Credibility is crucial. Having the credibility of being able to pull off successful collaborations is 100x more impactful than being a great competitor.

When you build your credibility as a collaborator, you won't even have to go out and find new collaborators because they'll find you. To a certain extent, you'll become the seller, not the buyer.

But don't assume that what you have to offer as a collaborator will suddenly be revealed in your collaboration. You have to go into a collaboration with someone else knowing what you bring to the table. Otherwise, no one is going to see you as an attractive potential collaborator. And you can't make assumptions about someone else's goals being resonant with yours.

It's vital that you go into a collaboration with complete knowledge of the value that both you and your collaborator are bringing to the endeavor and that you're both aligned on your audience and goals.

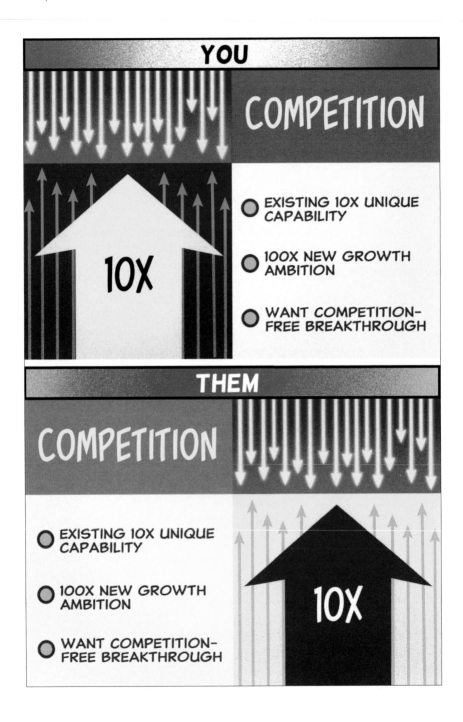

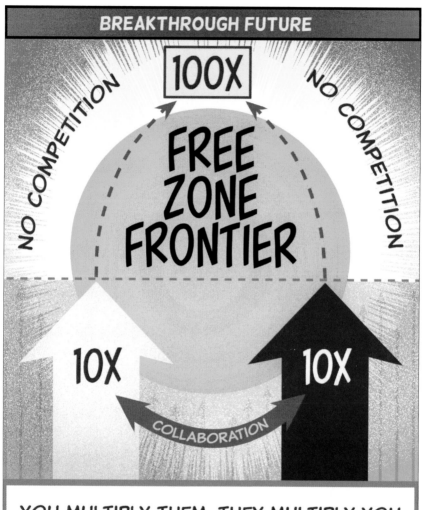

Chapter 2
Free Zone Creativity

You increasingly create new outside Free Zones by multiplying your current best capabilities with those of uniquely different innovators.

By its very nature, forging into a Free Zone can't be an independent activity. You can't be an isolated individual and create a Free Zone Frontier.

If you are, it just means you found a new way to spend time alone. But it doesn't create anything for anyone else. Free Zones start with an individual getting an idea about something, other individuals having resonant thoughts, and all of them saying, "Why don't we get together and team up?"

When one person launches into a new territory, it's only an opportunity if it creates opportunity for other people.

Thinking 100x higher.

I have to imagine that for early American settlers to get on a leaky ship and take an eight-week voyage across the Atlantic, they must have believed there was something extremely big on the other side.

To be motivated to launch into a new area and give up the security of what's already established, the possibility of a huge payoff is needed, one that can be measured. A goal like 100x.

If you take stock of what you have now, and figure out what 100x that would be, you can visualize the huge payoff it would be to grow your success by that much.

Focusing your 10x best.

You can set out for that new territory and that 100x payoff without greater internal cost or complexity, and without any loss of control over your personal and business quality of life.

You won't be selling or sacrificing what you've already achieved. You'll still own it 100 percent. You can think of what you've done so far as one single 10x capability, and now it can be creatively combined with others' 10x capabilities.

Your collaboration with someone else's 10x capability could be based on their technology, a new platform they've developed, a unique product or service they provide— anything that's a proven 10x achievement that will match up with your own 10x business to create something new in the marketplace.

You're not going back to what you've already created and trying to multiply inside of that. You're taking everything you've achieved and combining it with the achievements of others who have similar or resonant innovative ideas about a new territory.

"Free" outside multipliers.

What we're defining here is an entirely new dimension of entrepreneurism. If you go to business colleges, or to the most powerful entrepreneurial forums, nobody there thinks in this way. What we're talking about doesn't involve bring- ing in investors, or any of the customary things that require lawyers and contracts. It's simply about combining your capabilities with the capabilities of other individuals.

What holds it together is that both you and the individual you're collaborating with have a similar 100x ambition.

It's important to recognize that if you're in a true collaboration with someone, they aren't a competitor you have to defend yourself from. So if you find yourself in a discussion about engaging in a collaboration and then send a lawyer bearing a contract, you might have disqualified yourself from creating a Free Zone Frontier.

But if you're willing to take your 10x best capability and set out with similarly minded people for new territory, you can look forward to establishing and growing collaborations with an increasing number of ambitious achievers who provide you with their best 10x capabilities based on the agreement of mutually creating and sharing in a 100x future result.

Entirely new creation zones.
Every time you create a 100x collaboration through the combination of two or more 10x capabilities, entirely new markets and businesses can emerge.

You can only be part of this if you're being absolutely 100 percent of who you already are, which means your past is very important. You'll become aware of the full value of your past because now you get to use the entire achievement of your lifetime so far to take it much further.

But you're not doing it alone. And the truth is that you didn't get to where you are now without collaborating with other people, but there was no reason for you to see the power of that until you started treating your entrepreneurial company as a single capability.

Going 100x with your 10x capability isn't going to be 10x harder or 10x more work. It's going to be easier than that because you're going to be combining your *existing* capability with one or more capabilities of other people.

25 years fascinating.
In addition to a growth goal, you also need a time goal, so the same way that we're using 100x growth, we'll use 25 years.

To launch into something new, it has to have the potential of continually growing in an entirely new fashion for 25 years, and being exciting, fascinating, and motivating to you for all of that time.

And keep in mind that doing something for 25 years can't be about the money. Being ready to do this means that you've already gained the ability to finance yourself, and you're now looking at doing this for the excitement and the novelty of it.

If you don't see it that way, or the people you're considering collaborating with don't see it that way, there's no deal. But there's a very big population on the planet, and we have the ability to communicate electronically, so just by putting out a vision of something new, you can find all sorts of people who are similarly attracted to your idea.

You'll find that the new frontier of these Free Zones is so innovative and motivating that all of the 10x achievers who contribute their unique capabilities to their accelerating growth discover growing reasons to easily commit to them for 25 years.

CREATIVITY AND FREEDOM

Chapter 3
Competition-Free Frontiers

You continually expand your collaborative value creation in new ways so that existing competitors can't understand what you're doing differently.

When you're focused on competing with other people, you're using your biggest and best energies not to create new kinds of value but to try to make sure that no one gets ahead of you.

Competition isn't about the future; it's always about the past. It's wasting all of your energy worrying about losing what you already have. It's taking capabilities and getting the least value out of them by only trying to keep and protect what's already there.

If you're looking for a new opportunity to maximize the best of what you've already created, you can't do it by competing with what already exists.

Forgeting competitors forever.
If someone's a die-hard competitor who won't collaborate with others, there's no reason to pay them any mind. The goal is having 100x collaborations with similar-minded individuals.

As soon as you ignore what competitors are doing, you'll be energized to discover new frontiers where competitors will never be.

The only reward for entrepreneurs who have competitive mindsets is money, but in your situation, money is already taken care of.

When your goal is new opportunities in the realm of value creation, there will be immediate rewards in doing the activity itself. And new money will be attracted to your new ventures.

New, better, and different.

You now begin seeing all kinds of new value creation possibilities that are dramatically better because you're thinking, communicating, and achieving in an entirely different way.

Existing situations get crowded with people who think that competition is the way to get ahead, but it can't be.

And the way you get rid of competition is to just stop paying attention to it. Recognize that there isn't a scarcity of possibilities and resources, and just stop competing.

Something I've said for a long time is, "Innovate, don't compete," and it dates back to the early days of Strategic Coach when we allowed coaches outside of our organization to pay a fee to use our materials.

A couple of them got it into their heads that once they learned the materials, they'd no longer have to pay the fee, so it ended up being a mistake on my part to think that they were collaborators and not competitors.

We could have sued them, but I said, "I don't want to spend a cent on lawyers. I want to spend all of our money on creating brand new, better concepts and tools that make what they stole from us obsolete."

And that's what happened. They never created anything

from what they stole, but they got trapped by what they stole. Their whole focus became defending what they'd stolen, but since they hadn't created it in the first place, they had no way of improving it.

And their customers and clients would get to the frontier of what they'd stolen and find that there was nothing beyond that, and so their customers and clients would come to us.

They'd never think this way.

What those coaches did was provide me with instant motivation to create something new. Irritated oysters create pearls, and I said, "Let's turn all of this irritation into new things."

Instead of getting down about situations, or feeling competitive, you can use frustration as incentive to go where your competitors can't. The way to lose your competitors is to not think like them.

By simply ignoring your competitors, you've created a permanent way of thinking that's impossible for them to imitate because they always compare and compete.

Suddenly, you just disappear.

As soon as you bypass competition in your mind, your progress and achievements immediately disappear from the zone of competition.

Competitors no longer see you as competition, and they don't see any of the new breakthroughs you're having.

To entrepreneurs who don't recognize any reward other than money and ownership, what you're doing seems completely crazy. Unlike them, you recognize the many other rewards you can get from creation and collaboration, including capability, credibility, confidence, creativity, and connections.

But just as they stop thinking of you as a competitor, you're no longer paying attention to what they're doing. You're too busy innovating, creating new products and services, and discovering new Free Zones.

Innovate backward from free.
When people ask how they can become more innovative, I say, "Give up the whole thought of competition."

The fastest way to become innovative is to cut off copying and comparisons. Because when you do that, you'll have to look somewhere else. You'll have to look at the people who'd really love the new thing you're working on.

New frontiers and creative zones will materialize for you because you've permanently freed yourself to operate entirely outside of any kind of competition.

You've made a permanent decision to be free from competition, and so you suddenly become very innovative because now things can only be about the creation of new value.

It's no longer about winning against someone; it's only about creating something new.

And by its very nature, it will only be a big deal if it's valuable to other people, including your competitors.

Chapter 4
Instantly Invisible Advantages
You take extraordinarily profitable advantage of suddenly abundant situations that can't be seen in competitive circumstances.

In ordinary situations, an enormous amount of the profit you make has to be put toward competition. Because of this, competition is incredibly non-profitable.

Engaging in competition is a waste of your personal energies, personal capabilities, and the capabilities of your organization. You spend so much of your time shuffling for position in circumstances of scarcity and use up resources that you could instead be devoting to creativity.

When you create a new Free Zone, it's completely devoid of competition at first, and so it's incredibly profitable.

Abundant Free Zones.
These situations become suddenly abundant because you have an idea and then you and your collaborators define and create new Free Zones. It's all gain when it starts because the price is whatever you're charging. No one else is charging for it yet, so there's no comparison. The pricing mechanism of the marketplace isn't working there yet.

The price you set will be dictated by how quickly you want to grow the market, so you'll likely make it very reasonable so that as many people as possible can enjoy this new product or service you're offering.

But your emphasis is entirely on the new customers, not who's competing for your new customers, because there is no competition for them.

You can be more focused on your clientele, your creativity, and your innovations because there is room freed up in your brain now that you're no longer distracted financially or creatively by what other people are doing or worried about competition.

Seeing is creating.
From now on, all of your progress and growth can come from identifying Free Zones where entirely new value can be created using and multiplying the capabilities you already have. This maximizes the value of your experiences so far.

I think of things I did when I was around twelve years old, and I realize that I was preparing for what I do now as an adult without even knowing that that's what I was doing.

An existing capability I had was asking questions, and I used that as the basis for creating The Strategy Circle, a fundamental tool of The Strategic Coach Program.

Suddenly freed up.
Simply by changing your mindset to a new way of creating value for others, you free yourself up from the scarcity caused by conventional restrictions that hold everyone else back.

Most people are held back because they measure their success in comparison to others. That's a restriction because it doesn't have anything to do with your capabilities or with creating value for other people.

Abandoning thoughts of where you are in relation to other people frees you up to focus your energies and capabilities on the ideas you have that can be the most useful to others, and to measure how well you're doing in terms of your real, significant value to others.

Best possible game for you.

You'll clearly and confidently see new possibilities for value creation that will be the direct result of everything you've uniquely envisioned, attempted, and achieved in your life so far.

Your uniqueness comes from everything you've done. Everything that's been powerful, painful, frustrating, freeing, and so many more things all count. Your uniqueness, and what constitutes a Free Zone Frontier, are totally determined by how you've transformed yourself in the past.

Who you are is who you've evolved and transformed into. Since the game you're playing now is one that only you can play, with your unique capabilities and experiences, it's strictly your game. There can be no competition in it.

You can combine the summing up of your unique past with the summing up of someone else's unique past, using both of your capabilities to create something bigger, and there still won't be any competition whatsoever in that because each of you needs the other's capability that you yourself don't have.

Endlessly abundant.

As soon as you shift your thinking from the existing arena of isolated competition to the new Free Zone of ever-expanding collaboration with like-minded achievers, you won't believe how abundant the creative possibilities become.

Everything you've done in your past has made it possible for the next big, creative thing you're going to do. And this will always be true.

No matter how far you go, and how enormous your achievements are, you can always go beyond that because your experiences and achievements are now new or expanded capabilities that can be used for new, even bigger opportunities.

Opportunity, not status.

By increasingly developing and expanding new Free Zone Frontiers for the rest of your life, you'll bypass all considerations and concerns about your status in conventional circumstances.

This is a big deal, because the thing that we compete most for is status within what already exists. But competing for limited positions or resources is a scarcity mindset. And you're taking yourself out of these conventional circumstances.

You still have status—it's a collaborative status and a new value creation status. But you're not doing it for the status. Because if status is your goal, you'll eventually get all of the status you want and run out of opportunity.

There are systems that need to be maintained, and status is a good way to maintain certain systems—just not for you if you want to expand, transform, and use your capabilities in the best possible way to create new value for other people.

Chapter 5
Friction-Free Collaboration

You are now combining your 10x capabilities with those of a growing number of other 10x achievers to easily create entirely new 100x solutions.

Most really great entrepreneurs have become great in an environment of intense competition, where there's a high level of competitive pressure and price pressure.

That great capability can continue as it is if you keep doing what you're doing, but the big change comes from saying, "What if I take this 10x capability, and instead of just developing it, I look outside of what I'm already doing?"

The biggest possible growth will come from collaborations that combine your 10x capability with the 10x capability of someone who's in the same sort of position but in an entirely different industry.

Getting to 100x.

Combining your 10x capabilities with theirs is how you get to 100x, which would be impossible if you just continued playing the same game you were already playing.

You can't do it by yourself. What you're lacking is some particular capability, and you need to collaborate with someone who has that capability, who has the same mindset as you do, and who lacks a particular capability you have.

As soon as you've done it once, your way of looking at things changes, and you start seeing possibilities for more and more collaborations everywhere you look.

You can now recognize other potential collaborators, and

since you've proven yourself to be a collaborator, they can recognize you too.

Suddenly amazingly free.

Some entrepreneurs say that they really love competition, but I think that's just making a virtue out of a necessity. Since they think they'll always have to deal with competition, they do their best to turn it into a positive.

But when I've asked entrepreneurs how they'd really like things to be, they answer that they don't want to have any competition at all.

When you start to look beyond the competitive realm, you'll experience a sharp increase in opportunities to collaborate with other 10x achievers who are also looking to accelerate their progress by bypassing competition.

But it's important to remember that you're unlikely to find these collaborators within your own industry, because they're competitors. You might be able to join up and swap some business, but the collaboration won't be able to go 100x because you're still in the realm of competition.

10x capabilities everywhere.

Because you're committed to creating a Free Zone Frontier for your own 10x capabilities, your eyes and ears will identify countless other individuals who want to contribute to your endeavor.

Not every collaboration will necessarily be a major one, but after your first collaboration, you'll have "gone live," and you'll show up on collaborators' radars.

Before the first time you do it, you're just dreaming about it, but as soon as you've taken that step into the outside realm of collaboration, it creates an attractive energy and people want to join in. This is because many other individuals were dreaming about being collaborative just as you were.

Biggest, easiest jump ever.

If you compare this new Free Zone project with everything you've achieved up until now, you'll recognize that this will be, by far, the greatest single growth jump of your life.

This is because it doesn't require the same amount of effort to jump as you're used to. You're doing away with the gravity that's made you really work to get off the ground, and you can make bigger jumps on the moon than you can on Earth.

Making jumps in the collaborative world still requires effort, but it doesn't seem like much when compared to trying to do the same thing in the competitive world, and your efforts go further in this realm.

You already have what you need to make big, collaborative jumps happen: your existing 10x capability. You don't have to give anything up, you don't have to sell anything, and both you and your collaborator will benefit from the deal.

Compelling new value.

You don't get just one collaborator either. All of a sudden, there will be all sorts of collaborators you hadn't even seen before you took that first big jump in your growth by collaborating with someone outside of your industry.

By flouting the natural rules of competition, you'll find that anything that is resonant at all with collaboration will start coming to you. Everything you create in your new Free Zone Frontier will compel a growing number of other 10x creative collaborators to multiply the impact of what you're developing.

And there's no exchange of money between you. It's all just added value for everyone involved in the collaboration.

Past struggle seems small.
Every struggle and challenge you've experienced in the time it took to get to where you are right now will seem like a very small price to pay for the Free Zone rewards you're going to receive.

To continue to do what you've already done will create burnout and wear you down, and eventually, you'll run out of excitement about the future.

Not to mention, you've already been rewarded for your previous work—you have income, reputation, and status. It's time to move on to greater gains.

Some people will get to a certain point in their career and say they're too old for a change from what they've always done. They believe it's "a young person's game" to do something different.

But because of the Free Zone mindset, I feel younger than I did even 30 years ago. The Free Zone Frontier is a new level of entrepreneurism—and it's keeping me young.

Chapter 6
Escaping Crowded Conformity

Your growing Free Zone confidence enables you to escape from the downward pull of everyone else's limited results and expectations.

Actually creating value and receiving positive feedback makes up maybe only five or ten percent of the typical entrepreneur's existence.

The rest is made up of the problems that entrepreneurs face—practical, economic, psychological, and emotional—which all have to do with sometimes being successful but also failing a lot in the competitive business world.

In other words, entrepreneurs' negative stories tend to all relate to being in competition.

It can seem like competition is the center of the universe, but what if those entrepreneurs who've proven themselves as credible in the competitive world and are good at collaboration enter into an area where there's no struggle?

What you hoped might be true.
What may have seemed like fairy tale visions of your future that you kept to yourself during all of your years of competitive frustration and failure can actually take on a greater daily practicality than you ever imagined.

You can leave behind the negativity and feelings of scarcity that are such a big part of most entrepreneurs' lives. Everything can be positive, encouraging, and exciting. A future without competition is possible.

That's what a Free Zone is: a world without competition. New Free Zones don't last forever, but it's not your concern whether or when other people move into a Free Zone you've created. Your goal is just to create more and more Free Zones.

Bypassing all self-comparison.

As you continually develop and expand many different kinds of unique collaboration, you stop comparing any aspect of your life with anyone else's.

The only reason you've ever compared yourself to other people is that you were competing, and you can now be permanently in an environment of no competition.

Operating with a Free Zone Frontier mindset, what you're looking for in other people are unique capabilities you don't personally possess. You want to collaborate with them because they're unique, as you are, and their mindset resonates with yours because they also have a cooperative attitude.

Self-comparison means you're looking at yourself in relation to someone else. There's no value in doing this. It's not about value creation.

When you're trying to figure out how you can compete, you compare yourself, and you focus on best practices. Focusing on best practices tells you you're not into value creation but rather trying to be the same as everybody else.

It has nothing to do with creating something new. It's just

thinking, "What are the best people doing, and how can I be more like them?" That means you're trying to change everything in your company to match what already exists.

Instead, identify the area in which you're already ahead of the competition, package it, and go outside of the industry so there's no competition. And as soon as you go out there, you'll talk to people, asking, "If we match up our unique capabilities, what do you think we could do together?"

The person you'll talk to has likely already had the thought about going outside of their industry. It's the law of magnetism: People with resonant mindsets find one another.

Multiplying, not imitating.

In the Free Zone Frontier, there is no mimicking, imitating, or copying what competitors might do, but rather every unique 10x collaborator helps to multiply everyone else's creative contributions.

There's no actual value creation in doing what one of your competitors is doing, and people choose to do that only when they're in competition and aren't confident enough in their own value creation skills.

But it's not a factor in true collaboration, where you and another person are combining your best 10x capabilities to create something new. Copying anyone in this situation is just not necessary.

When you make the permanent move to the Free Zone Frontier, it means you've accumulated enough Free Zone capabilities that you're ready to play this different game, and all the people you're going to collaborate with have reached the same level. This means that no one playing this game is going to feel any need to "keep up" with anyone else. Instead, all of you are focused only on new value creation.

Increasingly gravity-free. You're no longer going to be weighed down by fatigue and costs of competitive strategies and activities.

Now, all of your greatest energy, concentration, and activities will be 100 percent utilized to create entirely new kinds of value in situations and circumstances that are completely different from any conventional marketplace.

You've already proven yourself in the competitive world as being someone with strong capabilities who's worth collaborating with, so now you need only engage with other people possessing strong capabilities who are also looking to leave competition behind.

Own it and grow it. Your entire personal future in an expanding universe of Free Zone Frontiers has a simple formula: As you take more responsibility for collaborating in a new way, you immediately feel the value growing for everyone involved.

You can't do this halfway. You have to have both feet in the Free Zone Frontier.

And you can't be irresponsibly collaborative. What you contribute and put out can't just be a cosmetic thing. It has to be real, from a genuine desire for new value creation, and you have to completely own it.

Chapter 7
Everything's Collaborative

You continually transform your best capabilities in ways that communicate you are easy to collaborate with.

Some people have capabilities that would be great for others to collaborate with, and they're constantly increasing their ingenuity and creative thinking, but they don't have a collaborative mindset.

There are many people who are stars at what they do, and they can't be beat in their field, but they don't play well with others.

In order to be a collaborator, you have to both recognize what your best capabilities are and appreciate the unique value of your collaborator's capabilities. Ultimately, someone who's easy to collaborate with is someone who's focused on always being useful.

Transforming backward.

When I was very young, I spent most of my time with adults, as I could learn from them, and I was allowed to tag along with them because I was interested in what they had to say and found ways to make myself useful to them whenever I could.

I differentiated myself from other children and experienced an extraordinary amount of freedom. Looking back now, I can recognize that what I experienced was a Free Zone. You can use your superior learning from your very first Free Zone, and every new one after that, as your guide and standard for improving the collaborative quality of everything else you'll achieve.

Once you've experienced a Free Zone while recognizing what it is, you can go back and detect any Free Zones you've previously had.

Easy growth, no friction.

You'll find that every time you collaborate—looking back, right now, and moving forward—it's easy. Growth and progress happen fast, and there's a shocking absence of frustration because there's no friction.

Suddenly operating friction-free is shocking at first because we're used to friction, to things not working, to struggle. As a matter of fact, the toughest thing for an entrepreneur can be to allow things to be easy.

A lot of entrepreneurs identify as people who can tough out obstacles, and so they end up *looking* for obstacles. They find meaning in resistance, and they have trouble comprehending the idea of having no resistance.

These kinds of ideas—that things have to be difficult—are reinforced in the media where it's believed that if there's no friction, there's no story. But stories like that aren't collaboration stories.

You have to have had the experience of friction-free collaboration before you have the standard you need to examine your experiences. And then experiences you've had can take on an entirely new meaning as you realize that times when you've been competing, you felt isolated and didn't like it, and the times you've collaborated have been easy, enjoyable, and energizing.

Appreciating Free Zone experience.

You'll find out that the obstacles just aren't there in Free Zones, and your understanding of the experience will deepen over time.

Every time you consciously compare collaborative experiences against competitive ones, you grow your awareness, knowledge, and appreciation of what being in a Free Zone feels like. The more you have the experience, the more you normalize it, and eventually you'll reach a point where not having the experience becomes abnormal.

When you were in the competition zone, you grew your muscle for that game by exercising it against resistance. Once you're in the collaboration zone, the resistance is gone and what you're growing are your collaboration capabilities.

Spotting other players.

The more you expand your lifetime understanding—both backward and forward—of how and where collaboration works for you, the more you'll be able to identify the collaborative capabilities and ambitions of other achievers who are easily accessible to you.

You have to have the awareness of the difference between collaboration and competition first. Otherwise, these potential collaborators could be all around you and you wouldn't spot them.

After all, our eyes only see and our ears only hear what our brain is looking for. And if your brain is convinced of the value and power of your collaborative experiences, all of a sudden you'll have active sensors that pick up the presence of a collaborative person.

And from then on, it can be nothing but pure collaboration for you—easy, fast, and friction-free.

Accelerating collaborator flow.

A byproduct of focusing on collaboration is that you get to know yourself better, identifying your best capabilities and how you can best contribute and be useful.

It's always who you already are inside that will enable you to create and multiply your competition-free collaboration projects outside of yourself.

The more you free yourself up from your scarcity-based competition mindsets, the more your new collaborative ambitions will speedily take you directly into a vast flow of other individuals' collaborative capabilities that are immediately more valuable than anything you could ever create on your own.

Competition is like swimming against the current, and collaboration is the opposite—you get a lot of help getting where you want to go. In many cases, we learn to compete before we really learn to think, and while there are reasons for this, it doesn't have to continue being your mindset.

It can be hard to divest yourself of all competitive thoughts and ambitions, but at a certain point, it's just baggage. And you don't have to keep on carrying it around.

You can unlearn things and shed the baggage of competition to move into your Free Zone Frontier where you can accomplish a lot more much more easily.

Chapter 8
Extending The Frontier

You realize that with your capability to collaborate on one Free Zone, you acquire the confidence to keep extending your frontier with further Free Zones.

Creating Free Zones is an addictive activity in the best sense of the word. As with any activity that's its own reward, the more you do it, the more you want to do it.

I'll use an analogy to do with physical fitness. Exercising makes you want to do more exercise, and the more exercise you do, the less you want to eat sugar. The more sugar you eat, the more sugar you'll want to eat, and the less you'll want to exercise. Both positive habits and negative habits perpetuate themselves.

Takes one to create two.

Your entire conscious jump from the competitive world to your first Free Zone Frontier requires only committing to your first 100x collaboration with a single other equally committed 10x achiever.

Once you've made this first collaboration and created your first Free Zone, the next one will be 10x easier and faster to put into place. It's a skill that multiplies itself.

The learning curve is very high the first time you do it because it's unfamiliar, but the very next time, you have an expectation of how it's going to go. You've learned what works, what doesn't work, and what to do better next time. Even if you get everything right the first time, it's still a tense exercise. Once you've done it 100 times and you've worked out a way that you can't get it wrong, that's a totally different capability.

And there's no way to start other than by getting out and collaborating to create your first Free Zone. It's by doing it that you'll develop different nerve endings and instant responses than what were necessary when you were in the competitive zone.

Competition forever over.

The shift from the long and heavy haul of isolated competition to an energizing future of endless collaboration is complete and total because once you're in your first Free Zone Frontier, your competitive past can be as behind you as you're willing to let it go.

For some people, it's difficult to leave their competitive pasts behind. They've done well enough in the competitive world to have the confidence and self-awareness needed for collaboration, but there's some part of it that they resist giving up.

It's like owning a Harley Davidson and still wanting the training wheels from your first bicycle. It's a crutch that isn't needed.

There's a sense of safety in sticking with what you're used to and what you know you excel at. If you're winning at the top of the competition game, moving on to the cooperative realm and pushing into new Free Zone Frontiers requires the willingness to supersede your ego and be a partner with someone else.

Momentum creates momentum.

While you're in your first Free Zone Frontier, you'll see that any and all additional collaborations to expand the Free Zone you're in, and all new Free Zones, always generate their own greater creative momentum for still further collaborations.

It's like a flywheel. All you have to do is get it in motion, and all further motion will be generated.

Other collaborators are watching you while you're in your first Free Zone, and they're thinking, "That person would be easy to link up with." They recognize that you too are a real player in the collaboration game.

Keep in mind that you can't understand every possible collaboration; you can only understand a collaboration that flows from your own unique capabilities. You can't see how unique capabilities you don't have would work in collaboration. You can only spot what would be needed for you to create 100x results. Otherwise, the amount of possibilities out there would just drive you crazy.

Everywhere you look, collaboration.

Your opportunistic eyes now only see, and your resourceful ears only hear, what your collaborative brain is looking for: For the rest of your entrepreneurial life, you'll only dream about, imagine, and visualize new kinds of Free Zone Frontiers and the specific, unique 100x collaborations that will create them.

You're never going to be looking for a general ability, only specific abilities that are necessary for you to collaborate with for your next Free Zone Frontier. I've seen it happen that someone becomes enthusiastic about collaboration but doesn't go about it in a strategic way, and they end up unhappily going back to the competitive zone.

The Free Zone Frontiers that you have the idea to create are always unique and specific, and so too are the other capabilities and collaborations that are needed to bring them about.

Always transforming upward.

While even your biggest and best competitive successes will gradually wear you down and eventually wear you out, in this new world of Free Zone Frontiers, every one of your new collaborative breakthroughs will transform your entrepreneurial capabilities and confidence to a new, higher level of creative energy.

You don't get worn out, you don't want to stop, and your ambition never gets smaller.

In my experience of coaching these concepts in workshops, people grasp them instantaneously. It's not a slow, trial-and-error process. Once people get it, their attitude becomes, "Why would I go about it any other way?"

You've already been conventionally successful. The way upward isn't staying on track, continuing to play that conventional game. The next step for you is transformation.

You'll be contributing and creating great value by using your best capabilities, but it won't be all about you. You'll be part of something greater: the collaboration world.

Conclusion
Collaboration Is The Center

You're shocked to realize that whereas you've always seen intense competition as the center of the entrepreneurial universe, you now see expanding collaboration creating Free Zone Frontiers as the center.

Imagine that there is a wall of intense competition around a competition-free zone, which is where you want to get to.

You want to jump over that wall and get right to the center, but at the same time, other people are fighting to prevent anyone from getting past them.

They're fighting to hold onto the competitive world they're familiar with, and the biggest strife to them is an unpredictable new form of collaboration that bypasses them. They can predict how others will compete with them because they themselves are master competitors, but this new form of collaboration doesn't use competitive skills, so it just blows right by them.

Competition can't compete with collaboration. By collaborating instead of competing, you're jumping right over that wall into the center, into the Free Zone.

Next entrepreneurial jump.
Over the course of your entrepreneurial career, as you were becoming more successful at competition, your greater progress and achievement were actually created by your growing ability to collaborate.

Being in an environment of competition doesn't have to be negative. It can be a pleasant experience if there are strict rules in it and you're properly trained in it. But it's limited. It doesn't create a bigger world other than a higher competitive world.

While you were competing, you became a better competitor, but the other part of the story is that you were getting better at collaborating. There's no place for collaboration stories, however, in a fiercely competitive world.

Now that you're ready to move up to the world of collaboration, you'll be bringing with you both your strong reputation as a competitor and your skills and ambition to be a creative collaborator.

Bypassing fear and fatigue.

Eventually, the pressures and demands of being competitive would worry you and wear you down, but using 100x collaboration to forge into new Free Zone Frontiers enables you to bypass the fear and fatigue that force most entrepreneurs out of the game.

Each year you're in the competitive zone leaves you with less energy and less motivation. And it's only getting more competitive out there. Think of phrases people throw around all the time like, "When the going gets tough, the tough get going" and "Go big or go home." It's an old, toxic game, and it's time to break out of it.

Keep in mind that turning yourself off from competition doesn't automatically mean you're collaborative. It can mean that you're aimless, and instead of having your own big vision, you're just part of someone else's big vision.

But going *toward* the world of collaboration as you turn away from competition means that you have 100x goals and visions. It's bigger vision and bigger value creation without all of the negative aspects.

Transforming every industry.
From the moment you collaborate to create your first Free Zone, you can see that this can be done anywhere, in every possible market and industry you encounter.

Once you figure out how the 100x collaboration and the creation of a Free Zone works, you can take that skill anywhere you want to move to. No matter what ends up interesting you later on, you can use that same model from your first conscious collaboration as you move into that new Free Zone.

Successful collaborations can often look from the outside like you've outcompeted somebody. But what really happened was that you collaborated to innovate something new that bypassed everyone in your industry or even transformed your industry.

You may have surpassed others in your industry whom you formerly saw as competitors, but that's a byproduct, not the purpose.

Abundant as you can collaborate.
Many of the feelings of scarcity you had in the past were caused by seeing yourself as an isolated competitor rather than as someone abundantly capable of collaboration.
It's a matter of having a micro versus macro perspective. If you're seeing only the relatively small world of competition,

it will seem to you as though there's a scarcity of available rewards. But if you're looking at the big picture in the world of collaboration, you'll get the sense that there's an abundance of rewards available.

Free Zone fascinating.

Everyone you meet who gets their first glimpse of how radically transformative it is to focus on 100x collaboration rather than competition will immediately want to bring every aspect of their future lives into alignment with creating greater Free Zones.

I did an exercise in one of my workshops where I said to my clients, "I want you to close your eyes and imagine your dream entrepreneurial future. What does that look like?"

Responses included "free of competition," "faster, easier, and cheaper," "abundant," and so on.

The truth is that no matter how much they may claim to love it, people who spend their entrepreneurial lives engaged in increasingly intense competition dream about a competition-free world where they can be truly innovative and collaborative.

And they're just one decision away from pushing forward into that new frontier.

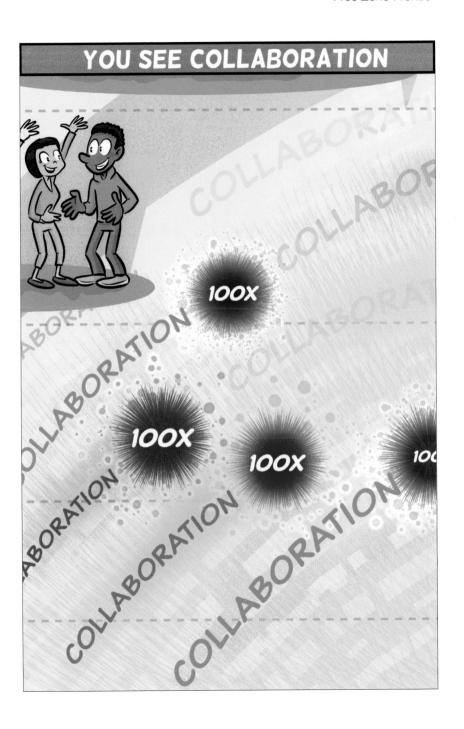

For Game-Changing Entrepreneurs

You commit to growing upward through three game-changing levels, giving yourself 25 years to transform every aspect of your work and life.

A lot of people might think they want to be a Game Changer, but they hope it will just happen for them. The Strategic Coach Program—a quarterly workshop experience for successful entrepreneurs—is for those who are committed and devoted to business and industry transformation for the long-term, for 25 years and beyond.

For many of them, this starts long before they're actually in business. They have an instinct about themselves and how they want to create their future that likely started in childhood. They've fought for their ability to control their time, to control how their money is made, to work with those they want to work with both inside their business and out in the marketplace, and there's a real purpose to their life, with the result that being buried inside of someone else's system could never be satisfactory.

If you've reached a jumping off point in your entrepreneurial career where you're beyond ready to multiply all of your capabilities and opportunities into a 10x more creative and productive formula that keeps getting simpler and more satisfying, we're ready for you.

Creating Free Zones.

The underlying concept of The Strategic Coach Program, WhoNotHow, is all about connecting and collaborating with the right "Whos" to achieve your goals. It involves asking yourself the right question when you come up with a new idea. Instead of asking yourself, "*How* can I do this?" ask,

"*Who* can do this?" You have to get rid of all "Hows" that prevent you from being collaborative by finding the right "Whos" to free you up.

It starts with collaborating with the right "Whos" inside your company to become superior within a competitive framework, and then a new game becomes possible where you collaborate with 10x "Whos" outside your company to create new Free Zones.

Three game-changing levels.

Strategic Coach participants continually transform how they think, make decisions, communicate, and take action based on their use of dozens of unique entrepreneurial mindsets we've developed. The Program has been refined through decades of entrepreneurial testing and is the most concentrated, massive discovery process in the world created solely for entrepreneurs who want to change their game.

Over the years, we've observed that our clients' development happens in levels of mastery. And so, we've organized the Program into three levels of participation, each of which involves two different ways of changing your game:

The Signature Level. The first level is devoted to coming to grips with your *personal game*, which has to do with how you're spending your time as an entrepreneur as well as how you're taking advantage of your personal freedom outside of business that your entrepreneurial success affords you. Upping your personal game before you move on to making significant changes in other aspects of your life and business is key because you have to simplify before you can multiply.

The second aspect of this level is how you look at your *teamwork game*. This means seeing that your future consists of teamwork with others whose unique capabilities complement your own, leading to bigger and better goals that constantly get achieved at a measurably higher rate.

The 10x Ambition Level. Once you feel confident about your own personal game and have access to ever-expanding teamwork, you can think much bigger in terms of your *company game*. An idea that at one time would have seemed scary and even impossible—growing your business 10x—is no longer a wild dream but a result of the systematic expansion of the teamwork model you've established. And because you're stable in the center, you won't get thrown off balance by exponential growth. Your life stays balanced and integrated even as things grow around you.

And that's when you're in a position to change your *market game*. This is when your company has a huge impact on the marketplace that competitors can't even understand. This is because they're not going through this game-changing structure or thinking in terms of 25 years as you are. Thinking in terms of 25 years gives you an expansive sense of freedom, while focusing on 90 days at a time within that framework gives you a remarkable sense of focus.

The Free Zone Frontier Level. Once you've mastered the first four types of "games," you're at the point where your company is self-managing and self-multiplying, which means that your time can now be totally freed up. At this stage, competitors become collaborators and it becomes an *industry game*. You can consider everything you've created as a single capability you can now match up with another company's to create collaborations that go way beyond 10x.

And, finally, it becomes a *global game*. You immediately see that there are possibilities of going global—it's just a matter of combining your capabilities with those of others to create something exponentially bigger than you could ever have achieved on your own.

36 mind-shifting core concepts.

With these three growth levels, there's a continual upward mastery of 36 mind-shifting concepts. These core concepts continually integrate with one another and evolve. Dozens more innovative concepts exist in the Program that support these core concepts.

Global game-changing community.

Entrepreneurism can be a lonely activity. You have goals that the people you grew up with don't understand. Your family might not comprehend you at all and don't know why you keep wanting to expand, why you want to take new risks, why you want to jump to the next level. And so it becomes proportionally more important as you gain your own individual mastery that you're in a community of thousands of individuals who are on exactly the same journey.

In The Strategic Coach Program, you benefit from not only your own continual individual mastery but from the constant expansion of support from and collaboration with a growing global community of extraordinarily liberated entrepreneurs who will increasingly share with you their deep wisdom and creative breakthroughs as Game Changers in hundreds of different industries and markets.

For more information and to register for The Strategic Coach Program, call 416.531.7399 or 1.800.387.3206, or visit us online at *strategiccoach.com*.

ENTREPRENEURS

FREE ZONE FRONTIER

25	26	27	28
29	30	31	32
33	34	35	36

10X AMBITION

13	14	15	16
17	18	19	20
21	22	23	24

SIGNATURE

1	2	3	4
5	6	7	8
9	10	11	12

WHO

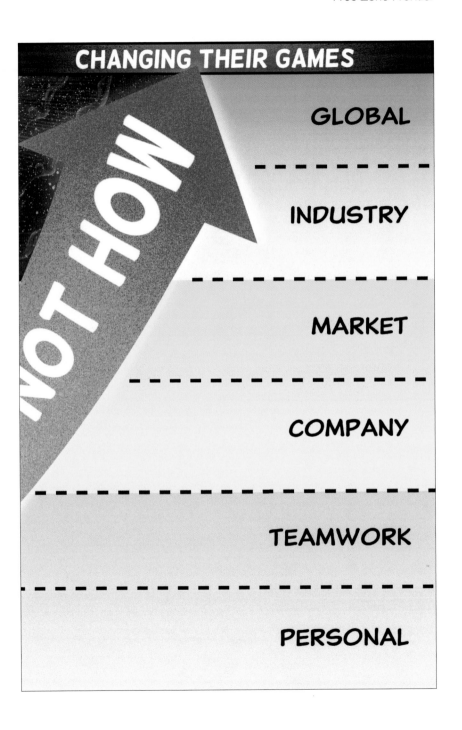

The Free Zone Frontier Scorecard

Turn the page to view the Mindset Scorecard and read through the four statements for each mindset. Give yourself a score of 1 to 12 based on where your own mindset falls on the spectrum. Put each mindset's score in the first column at the right, and then add up all eight and put the total at the bottom.

Then, think about what scores would represent progress for you over the next quarter. Write these in the second scoring column, add them up, and write in the total.

When you compare the two scores, you can see where you want to go in terms of your achievements and ambitions.

Mindsets	1	2	3	4	5	6
1 Creating Great Free Zones	You long ago lost any of your ability to be a successful competitor in both work and life and have no idea how you're going to cope.			You no longer believe that competition is a positive activity and are now open to new approaches that can permanently free you from it.		
2 Free Zone Creativity	You feel yourself increasingly trapped in a hopeless situation of increasing costs, regulation, and competition — with no escape.			You're bored with just doing okay with business as usual and want to transform your future with ideas that increasingly get better.		
3 Competition-Free Frontiers	You feel increasingly cut off and bypassed by competitors who are racing ahead with strategies and tactics that you don't see coming.			You realize that doing what everyone else is doing will never make you innovative, but you aren't sure yet how to jump ahead of everyone else.		
4 Instantly Invisible Advantages	You find it increasingly difficult to see any better possibilities for progress because no one is interested in what you can do.			You're not motivated to win the game that everyone else is playing because you know there's got to be a new, better game for you.		
5 Friction-Free Collaboration	You find that even your capabilities that others used to find acceptable are no longer seen as valuable in the unpredictable world around you.			You're finding a future trapped endlessly in increasing competition intolerable and are ready to transform everything to free yourself.		
6 Escaping Crowded Conformity	You now know that any dreams of a better life that you had in the past were fantasies, and you bitterly resent having been so deluded.			You realize that comparing yourself with others never works, and now all you want is to keep growing yourself to a higher level.		
7 Everything's Collaborative	Your fundamental attitude toward daily life and work makes it impossible for anyone to want to do anything with you in any situation.			You realize that your past failures and present frustrations come from your inability to collaborate, and you are committed to changing that.		
8 Extending The Frontier	You feel your future was over even before it started because you never understood how others managed to be confident, successful achievers.			You're frightened that you're losing energy and momentum and are motivated to create an energizing, more satisfying future.		
Scorecard	➡	➡	➡	➡	➡	➡

7	8	9	10	11	12	Score Now	Score Next
You have been fortunate and skillful at creating both a fixed occupation and lifestyle that are protected from competition.			You're always mastering the process of combining existing unique capabilities into a new venture that is automatically competition-free.				
You have a sustainably positive position in a predictable market where very little will need to be learned or invented.			You increasingly create new outside Free Zones by multiplying your current best capabilities with those of uniquely different innovators.				
You always change and improve your approach to match what your best competitors seem to be doing so you don't fall behind them.			You continually expand your value creation in new ways so that existing competitors can't understand what you're doing differently.				
You've worked long and hard to reach a level of success and status where nothing new is going to threaten your position.			You take extraordinarily profitable advantage of suddenly abundant situations that can't be seen in competitive circumstances.				
You're increasingly focused on holding onto and maintaining your present skill level, status, and lifestyle for as long as possible.			You are now combining your 10x capabilities with a growing number of other 10x achievers to easily create entirely new 100x solutions.				
You have always had reasonable and acceptable goals that you've achieved in ways that are now raising you to an admired status.			Your growing Free Zone confidence enables you to escape from the downward pull of everyone else's limited results and expectations.				
You have mastered all the processes that now make you successful and satisfied where you are, and no new learning is needed.			You continually transform your best capabilities in ways that communicate you are easy to collaborate with.				
You realize that everything that lies ahead in your life has to be focused on protecting and preserving what you have already achieved.			You realize that with your capability to collaborate on one Free Zone, you acquire the confidence to extend your frontier with further Free Zones.				
➡ ➡ ➡ ➡			➡ ➡ ➡ ➡				

About The Author
Dan Sullivan

Dan Sullivan is the founder and president of The Strategic Coach Inc. and creator of The Strategic Coach® Program, which helps accomplished entrepreneurs reach new heights of success and happiness. He has over 40 years of experience as a strategic planner and coach to entrepreneurial individuals and groups. He is author of over 30 publications, including *The 80% Approach*™, *The Dan Sullivan Question*, *Ambition Scorecard*, *Wanting What You Want*, *The 4 C's Formula*, *The 25-Year Framework*, *The Game Changer*, *The 10x Mind Expander*, *The Mindset Scorecard*, *The Self-Managing Company*, *Procrastination Priority*, *The Gap And The Gain*, *The ABC Breakthrough*, *Extraordinary Impact Filter*, *Capableism*, *My Plan For Living To 156*, *WhoNotHow*, *Your Life As A Strategy Circle*, and *Who Do You Want To Be A Hero To?*, and is co-author with Catherine Nomura of *The Laws of Lifetime Growth*.